MY FIRST HALLOWEEN

High Contrast Baby Book for Newborns

KREATIVE ART PRESS

By Kreative Art Press

For More Visit Us At : https://www.amazon.com/~/e/B08W4QFZWM

HAPPY HALLOWEEN

Dear customer ,thank you for Purchasing this book
We always welcome your reviews and suggestions
on our amazon page, your feedback is highly appreciated

RIP

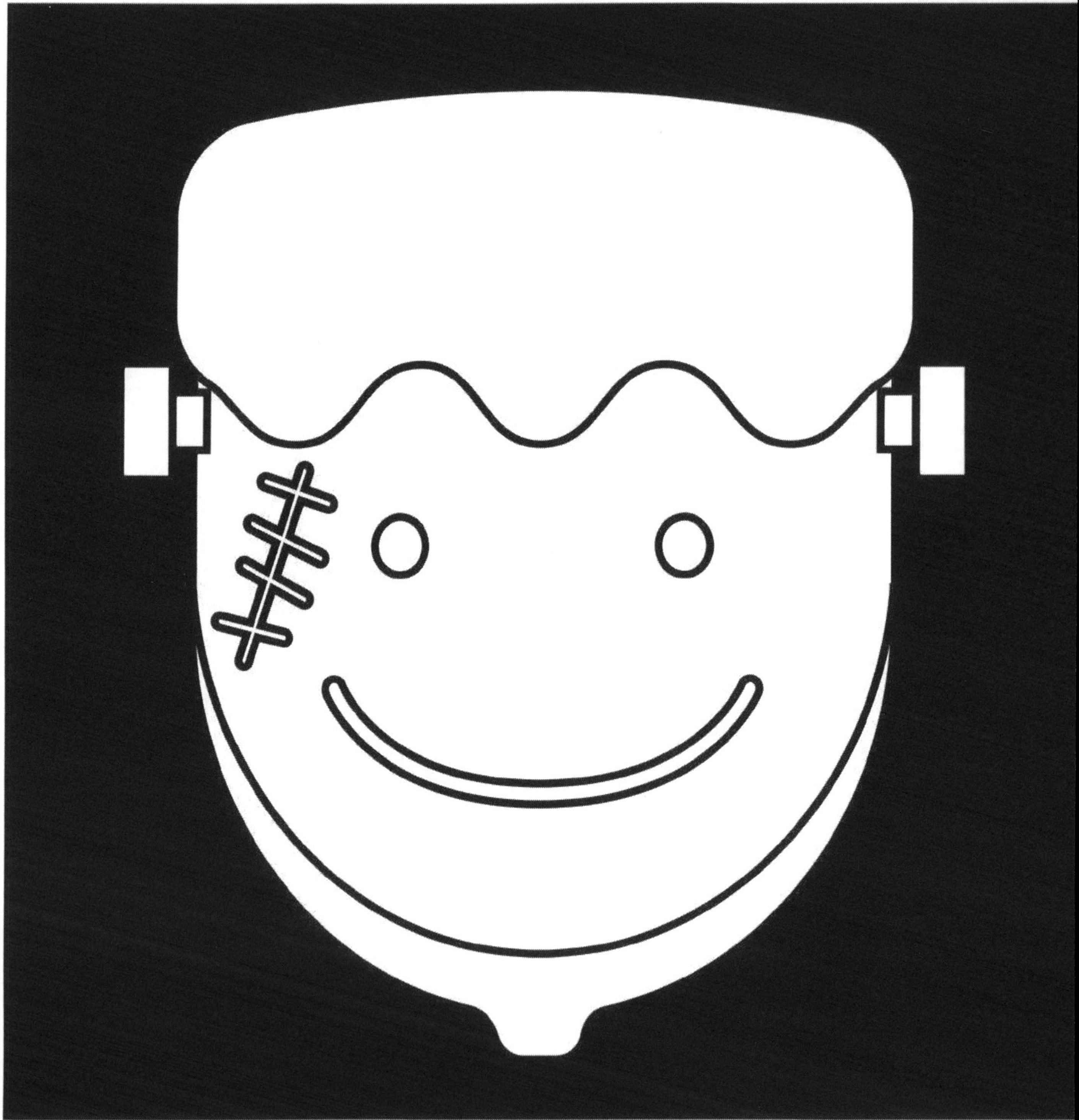

Printed in Great Britain
by Amazon

29524340R00024